DRAGONFLY

I am **not** a dragon.
And I am **not** a fly.
I am a . . .

DRAGONFLY

written by
Emery Bernhard

illustrated by
Durga Bernhard

HOLIDAY HOUSE · NEW YORK

For Gary and Regina

Library of Congress Cataloging-in-Publication Data
Bernhard, Emery.
Dragonfly / written by Emery Bernhard ; illustrated by Durga
Bernhard. —1st ed.
p.   cm.
Summary: An introduction to the physical characteristics,
life cycle, natural environment, and relationship to humans
of the dragonfly, considered to be among the most beautiful insects
in the world.
ISBN 0-8234-1033-1
1. Dragonflies—Juvenile literature.   [1. Dragonflies.]
I. Bernhard, Durga, ill.   II. Title.
QL520.B47   1993   92-39930   CIP   AC
595.7'33—dc20

Special thanks to Michael P. Kambysellis, Professor of
Biology, New York University, for his comments on the text
and artwork

Its face is fierce, and some people even think it looks like a little dragon . . . but a dragonfly is an insect.

Dragonflies were soaring through the air one hundred million years before dinosaurs walked the earth. Their wings measured up to 33 inches across. They were the largest insects ever.

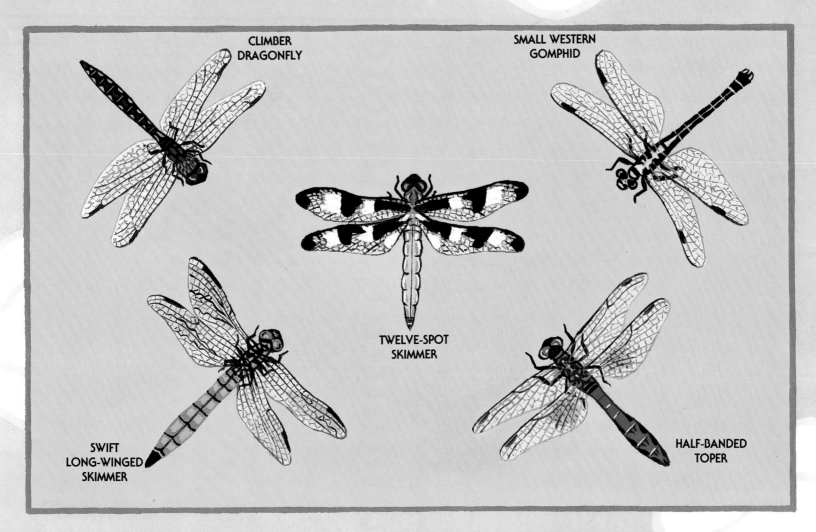

CLIMBER
DRAGONFLY

SMALL WESTERN
GOMPHID

TWELVE-SPOT
SKIMMER

SWIFT
LONG-WINGED
SKIMMER

HALF-BANDED
TOPER

Today, dragonflies have wingspans ranging from 1 to 7 inches. There are about 5,000 types of dragonflies in the world, including more than 400 kinds in North America. Dragonflies are many different sizes and colors. They are among the most beautiful of all insects.

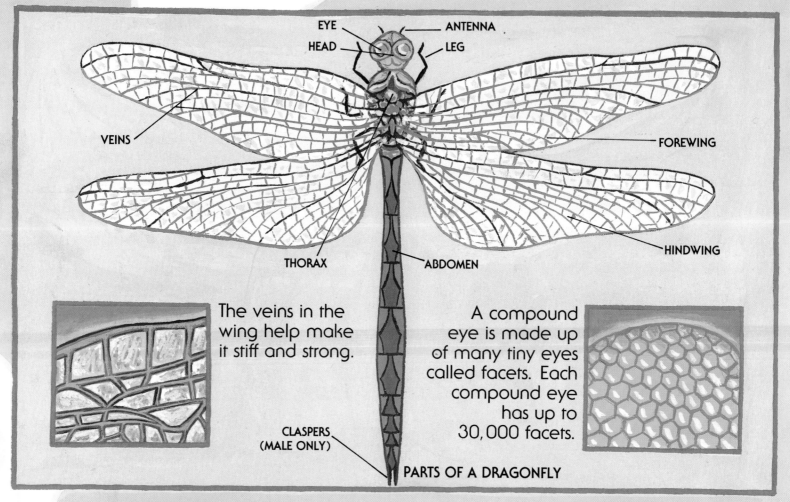

EYE
ANTENNA
HEAD
LEG
VEINS
FOREWING
HINDWING
THORAX
ABDOMEN

The veins in the wing help make it stiff and strong.

A compound eye is made up of many tiny eyes called facets. Each compound eye has up to 30,000 facets.

CLASPERS (MALE ONLY)

PARTS OF A DRAGONFLY

Like all insects, the dragonfly has a head, thorax, and abdomen. Its body is covered and protected by a hard, shiny outer skin. The abdomen is long and thin. The thorax has three pairs of legs and two pairs of wings. A dragonfly can swivel its head around and see in all directions. With its two enormous eyes, it can see as far as 42 feet.

Dragonflies are daring fliers, swooping and darting after their prey. They can zoom along at 35 miles per hour or hover in mid-air like a helicopter.

When a dragonfly sights its prey, its spiny legs form a kind of basket. It zigzags through the air, using this bristly basket to scoop up mosquitoes, flies, gnats, and bees.

The dragonfly munches on its prey as it flies, crunching up small insects with powerful jaws. After a meal a dragonfly may land and clean its face with the tiny bristles on its front legs.

Dragonflies can usually dodge the birds, frogs, and fish that attack them. But when the weather is too cold, a dragonfly cannot fly. Then it may scare away an enemy by raising its abdomen and flicking its wings.

Dragonflies usually mate in the summer. Many kinds of males set up territories and chase away other males that enter. The male has two claspers on the end of his abdomen. When a female flies into his territory, he grasps the back of her head with his claspers. Then the male and female connect their abdomens.

After mating, the female is ready to lay her eggs. She may drop them directly into water or push them into water plants. Male dragonflies often protect the eggs by flying along with their mates while the eggs are being laid.

Some dragonflies lay hundreds of eggs, others lay thousands. Each egg is slightly smaller than the top of a pin.

Dragonfly eggs usually hatch after about three weeks. The tiny wingless creatures that wriggle out are called nymphs. They breathe through gills inside the rear of the abdomen. As the nymphs crawl over the bottom of a pond or stream, they are sometimes eaten by frogs, water beetles, and other enemies.

Dragonfly nymphs are a dull color that blends in with the background and makes them hard to see. They hide in the mud or in the water weeds, waiting for their prey. Young mosquito larvae are their favorite snack.

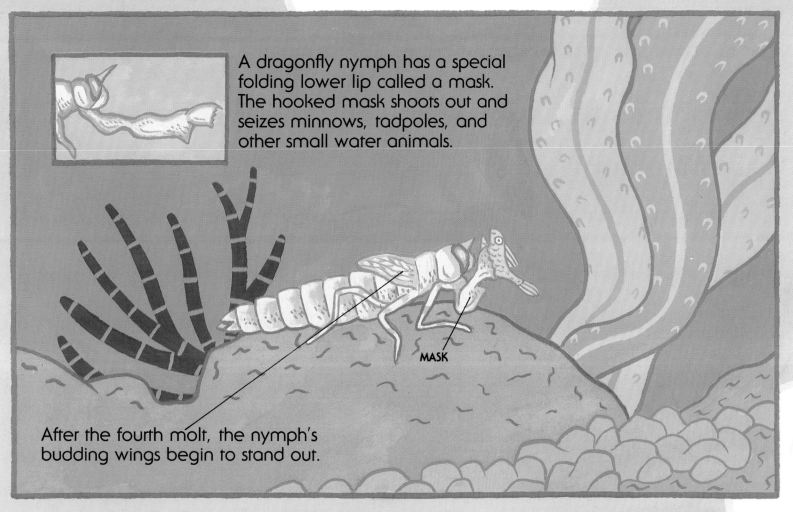

A dragonfly nymph has a special folding lower lip called a mask. The hooked mask shoots out and seizes minnows, tadpoles, and other small water animals.

MASK

After the fourth molt, the nymph's budding wings begin to stand out.

The nymph eats and grows. As it grows, it sheds its outer skin. This is called molting. Depending on the climate and the type of dragonfly, a nymph molts ten to sixteen times. Nymphs remain in the water from three months to five years before changing into adults.

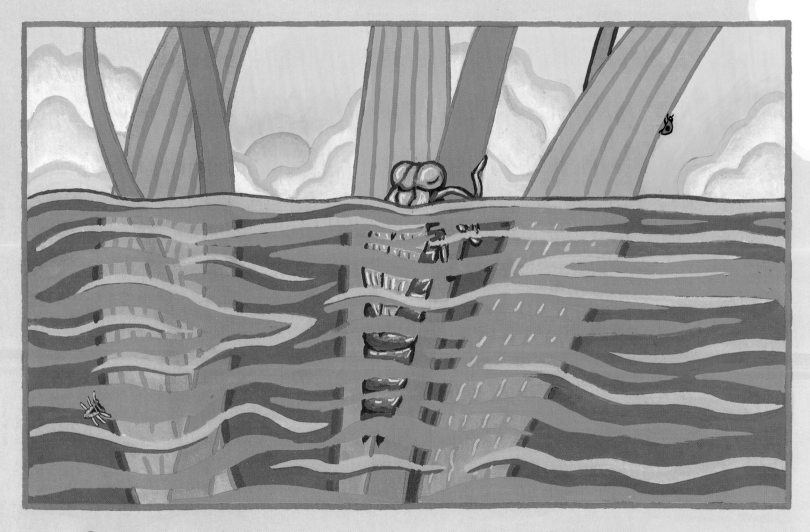

One warm afternoon, when the nymph is full grown, it climbs up toward the light and air. With its head barely out of the water, the nymph stops and waits for sunset.

MOLTING

Then, under the cover of night, the nymph clambers out of the water. It is ready to become an adult. The dragonfly molts for the last time, its old skin splitting open so it can struggle free.

The wings of the dragonfly unfold. At first, they are small, soft, and wet. The dragonfly pumps blood into the veins in its wings. This makes them expand. Now the dragonfly must wait until its wings harden and dry. In the light of day, a bird or frog might catch a dragonfly that can't fly. It must be ready to fly by dawn.

And it is ready! . . . The dragonfly stretches out its wings and beats them up and down, faster and faster. At sunrise it flies for the first time.

Dragonflies mate just a few weeks after they take to the air, and they die soon after they mate.

Dragonflies never hurt people. Sometimes they even help people by catching insects that sting or bite. In its short life a single dragonfly can eat thousands of mosquitoes and flies.

People help dragonflies by saving wetlands and by keeping the water clean where dragonflies need to live.

Over the centuries, people have thought about dragonflies in different ways.

In ancient times, Japanese farmers believed the dragonfly was the spirit of the rice plant. Dragonflies were a welcome sign of a good rice harvest.

Dragonflies were also believed to bring good luck in battle. About 1600 years ago, the dragonfly was the symbol of a great Japanese warrior clan. The dragonfly later became one of the emblems of the emperor. An old name for Japan—*Akitsu-shimu*—means Dragonfly Island. The dragonfly is praised in many Japanese poems and songs.

The Mimbres people of the American Southwest painted the dragonfly on ceremonial pottery as a symbol of life.

The Zuñi tell an ancient story of a magic dragonfly made from corn and straw. It came to life in a time of drought and famine, became a messenger to the gods, and helped save the people.

But not everyone has liked dragonflies. In Great Britain, they were once considered evil and dangerous. Because people saw them darting at horses, dragonflies were called "horse-stingers." They didn't realize the dragonflies were snatching horseflies—the real "horse-stingers."

In the lake country of northern Canada, blackflies can bite in annoying swarms. People are happy when dragonflies appear in midsummer because they feed on the flies.

If you walk near a pond early one summer morning, you might find a dragonfly resting among the leaves. It may be waiting for the sun to warm its body and dry its wings. Maybe you'll be lucky and get close, though the dragonfly is shy and hungry, and will soon take to the air . . .

Good-bye!

GLOSSARY

abdomen (AB-doh-men): The rear section of an insect's body.

claspers: A pair of graspers at the tip of the male dragonfly's abdomen.

gill: An organ that takes oxygen from the water so that an animal can breathe underwater.

insect (IN-sekt): A small animal with three main body parts, three pairs of legs, and usually one or two pairs of wings.

larva: The wingless, wormlike form of an insect that hatches from the egg.

mask: The hinged lower lip used by dragonflies to catch prey.

molt: When an animal sheds the outer covering of its body.

nymph (nimf): The special stage between egg and adult in dragonflies and other insects, in which the larva develops wings and may live underwater.

prey (pray): An animal that is hunted by another animal for food.

thorax (THOR-ax): The middle section of an insect's body, to which two pairs of wings and three pairs of legs are attached.

vein (vayn): In the nymph stage, a vessel that carries blood to the wings. In the adult stage, a threadlike structure that stiffens the wing and no longer carries blood.

wetland: A swamp, tidal flat, or other damp area of land that is home to many kinds of plants and animals.